Rebuilding

Mairi Innes

BookLeaf Publishing

India | USA | UK

Presentation by *BookLeaf Publishing*

Web: www.bookleafpub.com

E-mail: info@bookleafpub.com

ISBN: 9789360945053

First edition 2024

For Elléa and Sienna-my little loves.

When Again

You turn to me
And sleepily, luxuriously ask
"When again?"
Casual, off-hand.

I pause just long enough
To bite my tongue from answering
Too quickly.
Avoiding eagerness,
When all I want to say is

"Is the very next second
Too soon?"
Will I blink and like a daydream
You'll be gone? This feels too
ethereal
Too warm and inviting.

The (Sub)Text

"Hey, I think you are
a really nice girl,"
(A greater insult there never was.
I'd rather be
Cruel, cutting,
Conniving
A real cad,
Than simperingly nice-
Devoid of any persona.
But you didn't
Ask about me anyway.)

"but I don't think
we should keep dating."
(24 hours ago we laughed
Til tears sparked our eyes.
I made you a meal-
Apologetic, fearful
I'd done too much.
I've never been good
At playing it cool.)

"I'm still not sure
what I want"
(Perhaps I can help.

Someone thinner
With better skin.
Someone cooler
Someone you have to
Win.)

"and I need
To find it out."
(Swipe right
On more faces:
Empty vessels.
See your own ego
Projected back
In their hopeful eyes.)

"I really hope
you find
someone
who is right for you."
("Someone more
Your level:
Below me.")
 x

Sunshine

You used to call me your sunshine.
It had been so long
Since someone saw me:
Bright, gleaming,
Radiant.
Back then
Your warmth for me mirrored
My sunny disposition.
A gilded age for us.

I never fully reckoned with
The truth behind this moniker.
Pet name is perhaps
More accurate:
You wanted me docile,
Shiny, eager to please,
Subservient. I didn't understand then
What I see now:
Here, the sun remains behind the clouds.
All too often, thunder threatens
To chase the sun from the sky
All spark of light
Doused.

Your grey days permeated me
Stole my shimmer, dulled the sparkle
In my eyes.
What a lesson to learn:
You can't create a rainbow
When someone else only sees the rain.

The Thief

In school we learn that
"Like" and "as" create comparison.
"Spot similarities with the world around you
To elevate your writing."

Yet "just as" these words compare ideas
"So too" do they confine them:
individual concepts, birds trapped
In claustrophobic rooms, wings beating
Against the pecked glass window
Of a balanced sentence.

As we learn this skill of judging this to that
Seeking likeness, affinity, a whole-
The converse naturally creeps in.
Sinking doubt of a teenage mind:
My body, not "just as", but "more so"
So too, the comparison
Overshadows originality.
"Why can't I be just as
Normal as the rest?
I'm just so, just too
Much."

Here the thief takes hold
Comes in at midnight, turns naivety
To knowledge. Takes the ignorance,
The individuality
Of youthful joy
And leaves in its place
The spectre of shame.

Weaponised Weeping

You perceived my tears
As warfare: acid rain
Deliberately dripping down
On your perfect argument.
I could never comprehend
Your vitriol; the immediate escalation
To rage when my tear ducts betrayed me.

My tears blinded you
To my distress, genuine pain:
"Stop being so manipulative,"
You spat, the venom as unconscious
As my cries.

"Big boys don't cry"
And yet I can:
the disparity tormented you.
You couldn't convey your
Frustration except through bile,
Verses of curses cutting me down
To size.

The realisation took time
To thaw out, seep into the reason
Centre of my mind.

I was never scheming,
But I planned my escape.
Now, when my eyes smart
And fill, I embrace the emotion:
Weaponised weeping.

A Seat At The Table

The kitchen table at my parents' home
is my lifeboat.
There, I am steady when all around me
Crashing waves threaten to overpower.
The bubbling bluster of the kettle
Settles my soul, tells me peace is coming-
With biscuits, too.

I've sat at this table since I was 4:
Pudgy limbs dangling, food smeared
Across my chin.
When I return I am child again:
Protected and comforted,
Well-fed and soothed.

The mundane everyday is etched
Into the surface of the wood
By our voices. No historian would take note
Of the tears, the giggles, the terse words
Transcribed into the oak-our family language,
Our nest of nonsense.

Mum hovering over the stove,
Dad warm beside the radiator:
There is calm in the quotidian.

Women's Survey

Have you ever
Scrambled at your door,
Scratched your key at the lock
Feet tapping at the floor
Heart running amok?

Have you ever
Dreaded the ding of a phone
The message of hate
Felt frightened alone
Of coming back late?

Have you ever
Looked back in the street
Once, twice, again-be sure,
Desperate not to meet
His face? Quick, check once more.

Have you ever
Placated, reassured, soothed,
An open threat, a live grenade
Ready to fight, can't be moved
From the chaos he has made?

Have you ever
Been "asking for it?"
"Come on, don't play hard to get."
"Who cares-you're not even that fit."
"The biggest slut I've met."

Have you ever
Cried silent, muffled tears
Praying tomorrow will bring change?
No more jeers, no more fears
Wouldn't that be safe and strange?

Break Up Haiku

It's not me, it's you.
We're taking different paths now:
Yours is more downhill.

I just need some space.
We can still be friends; maybe
Online, or by pigeon.

I must work on ME-
The spark has sadly fizzled.
I wish you the best.

You Could Be So Pretty

You could be so pretty
If
Pretty was a superlative
Higher than beautiful,
Stunning,
Mesmerising.

You've got a lovely face
But
Let me tell you about your spirit:
The warmth it casts over others,
They shine in your rays.

You're a really lovely person
Yet
You're also direct, assertive,
Unafraid to speak your mind.
Self-assured.

I think you're brilliant
However
The real meaning:
"Intense brightness of light"-
You are.

My Phone is a Horror Film

MY phone is a horror film
In my messages, zombies and ghosts.
The graveyard of lost men
Comes alive at night to boast.

Social media vampires-
On schadenfraude they feed.
Glittering in the eerie glow
Of their finely curated feats.

In carefullly catalogued photo albums
Haunted memories lurk.
Spectres from the past await,
Observing sad sighs with a smirk.

The camera is a hall of mirrors
Distorting before my eyes.
Filters to flatter or frighten,
To taunt or terrorise.

My thumping heart races
At the work email jump-scare.
Doomscrolling the news in bed,
I invite vivid nightmares.

The shrill alarm blares
From scams and con artists.
The call is coming
From outside of the contact list.

Dating app werewolves
Transform at the moon's blue light
"Heeeeeere's Johnny!"
Hey, I thought I blocked him last night?

I think it might be watching me:
It stalks every move I make.
(For my health, of course-
Those 10k steps I must take.)

My phone is a horror film
Though I can't deny-one I have made.
I can't tear my eyes away from the screen:
Be afraid, be very afraid.

On Singledom

What if it's just you?
This is it:
Waking up, stretching
Out, taking up
Space.

What if it's silent?
No "good morning",
"Hello, you".
The footsteps upstairs
Your first contact.

What if it's empty?
A calendar clean of
Responsibilities.
A whole weekend ahead
Hours of you alone.

What if it's possible?
Enjoying the space,
The time,
The silence?
What if it's freedom?

Girl, Gone

If I go missing
All photos from ages
11 to 17
Are embargoed from the
Inevitable documentary
Series.

When they interview you
Some key points to review:
"She was always so thoughtful;
Her kindness knew no bounds.
Who would ever harm
Such a charming, meek
Humble individual?"

Whatever you do
Don't allow the crew
To look at my podcast
History.
"She Gone Girled herself,"
They'll assume.
Hey, we all have
Our niche interests.

I must request

At my behest
Do not share
Any voicenotes recorded.
Protect the innocent (me)
From further victimisation
(By my drunken screeching
Self.)

If I go missing
Consider a gentle
Photoshop or flattering filter.
I may be gone
But let's assume
There might be a man out there
To find me.

Exchanges

When does comfort turn to
Cloying, claustrophobic?
A sense of closeness that
Presses down on you,
Suffocating, stifling
Your voice.

Idolisation devolves
To possession.
A puppet with tangled strings,
Failing to perform precisely.

Sweet nothings twist to barbs
Honeyed words were designed
To entrap and subdue.
I should have anticipated
Each sharp bee sting.

When does security
Trump self-esteem?
What are you willing to trade
To feel acceptance?

Whisper It

In the quietest of moments,
Under the covers,
Late at night-
I allow my mind to drift
To you.

I think about how it was
When it was new; when we reached
New milestones. Discovering
The world together was
Exciting at 25; less so
Alone at 33.

I breathe in the 'what ifs'
The ones that smothered me
When we first parted.
In the light of day
I can dispel them;
Rationalise the reasons
Why it would never work.

But just for now
In this private, fleeting moment
I dream of you.

Cinema

I like it here:
Hushed, reverent,
Transfixed on the present moment.

I disconnect:
My phone, my worries,
My everyday burden.

The lights fade:
A collective rush,
Flutter of anticipation.

The film plays:
We feel possibility,
We might witness greatness.

Girls Like Mystery

I'm trying to create my own character,
Trying to make her seem interesting.
No, not interesting-
Mysterious.

I want people to wonder:
"who is that mystery lady
Drinking chai and reading?"
I want them to think:
Solitary, sophisticated.

I want to sit alone at a bar,
Glass of red wine in hand
And no distractions.
I want to be approached
By the intrigued
(but only if they're
Handsome men.)

I want to be so watchably unaware
Someone photographs me candidly.
They post it on Instagram:
A million likes.
I want them to think:
"What kind of life does she live?"
Oblivious to the
Painstaking pretence.

The Woman Before

My heart aches for the women
Who came before me:
Vulnerable and fragile in ways
I have always been protected from;
Ways he could exploit.

I am not stronger,
Not braver or any other
Superlative. I am fortunate.
I am surrounded by care,
Wrapped in so much love
I could see what was missing.

What is 9 months to 11 years?
I think of her often; how he painted her
As broken, unstable, unfit.
The shame I now feel for dismissing her
With pity, rather than empathy.

What sisterhood can be sought
In shared degradation?
All I know is
If I could hold your hand, apologise for
The unspoken judgement
I would.

In Sickness and In Health

(For Fiona and Douglas-14/05/22)

For most
It's a hypothetical:
Endless cups of tea on demand;
A box of tissues delivered at speed;
The comforting touch of a caring hand;
Holding your hair over the toilet in need.

For us, it's visceral:
It's staring into the ugly reality
That life isn't easy.
"Health is wealth" is never more true
Than when you're scrambling for pennies;
Praying for a lottery win.

The Japanese have kintsugi:
The art of mending the broken
By pouring gold into the cracks.
Sometimes our flaws, our weaknesses
Allow the other to shine
To be our strength, to make us whole again.

As we say those precious vows today,
Take time to reflect on the words.

How true: "In Sickness and in health" binds us,
And yes, "until death do us part".
But now we deserve to do some living
And here and now is where we start.